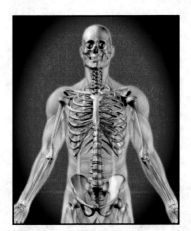

CELLS, SKELETAL SYSTEM & MUSCULAR SYSTEM
Human Body Series

● ●

Written by Susan Lang

GRADES 5 - 8
Reading Levels 3 - 4

Classroom Complete Press

P.O. Box 19729
San Diego, CA 92159
Tel: 1-800-663-3609 / Fax: 1-800-663-3608
Email: service@classroomcompletepress.com

www.classroomcompletepress.com

ISBN-13: 978-1-55319-378-4
ISBN-10: 1-55319-378-4

© 2007

Critical Thinking Skills

Cells, Skeletal System & Muscular System

Skills For Critical Thinking	Reading Comprehension								Hands-on Activities
	Section 1	Section 2	Section 3	Section 4	Section 5	Section 6	Section 7	Section 8	
LEVEL 1 Knowledge									
• List Details/Facts	✓	✓	✓	✓	✓	✓	✓	✓	✓
• Recall Information	✓	✓	✓	✓	✓	✓	✓	✓	✓
• Match Vocabulary to Definitions	✓	✓	✓	✓	✓	✓	✓		
• Define Vocabulary					✓			✓	
• Label Diagrams		✓			✓				✓
• Recognize Validity (T/F)				✓			✓	✓	
LEVEL 2 Comprehension									
• Demonstrate Understanding	✓	✓	✓	✓	✓	✓	✓	✓	✓
• Explain Scientific Causation			✓	✓				✓	
• Describe	✓	✓	✓		✓	✓		✓	✓
• Classify into Scientific Groups	✓	✓	✓	✓			✓		
LEVEL 3 Application									
• Application to Own Life	✓		✓	✓		✓	✓		✓
• Organize and Classify Facts			✓						
LEVEL 4 Analysis									
• Make Inferences			✓				✓		✓
• Draw Conclusions Based on Facts Provided			✓	✓		✓	✓		
• Classify Based on Facts Researched	✓	✓	✓						✓
LEVEL 5 Synthesis									
• Compile Research Information	✓	✓	✓	✓	✓	✓			✓
• Design and Application									✓
• Create and Construct									✓
• Ask Questions	✓				✓	✓			✓
LEVEL 6 Evaluation									
• State and Defend an Opinion				✓		✓	✓		
• Defend Selections and Reasoning						✓	✓		

Based on Bloom's Taxonomy

Contents

● ● ● ● ● ● ● ● ● ● ● ● ● ● ● ● ●

Assessment Rubric

Cells, Skeletal System & Muscular System

Student's Name: _____ Assignment: _____ Level: _____

	Level 1	Level 2	Level 3	Level 4
Understanding Concepts	Demonstrates a limited understanding of concepts. Requires teacher intervention.	Demonstrates a basic understanding of concepts. Requires little teacher intervention.	Demonstrates a good understanding of concepts. Requires no teacher intervention.	Demonstrates a thorough understanding of concepts. Requires no teacher intervention.
Analysis & Application of Key Concepts	Limited application and interpretation in activity responses	Basic application and interpretation in activity responses	Good application and interpretation in activity responses	Strong application and interpretation in activity responses
Creativity and Imagination	Limited creativity and imagination applied in projects and activities	Some creativity and imagination applied in projects and activities	Satisfactory level of creativity and imagination applied in projects and activities	Beyond expected creativity and imagination applied in projects and activities
Application of Own Interests	Limited application of own interests in independent or group environment	Basic application of own interests in independent or group environment	Good application of own interests in independent or group environment	Strong application of own interests in independent or group environment

STRENGTHS:

WEAKNESSES:

NEXT STEPS:

Teacher Guide

Our resource has been created for ease of use by both TEACHERS and STUDENTS alike.

Introduction

This resource provides ready-to-use information and activities for remedial students in grades five to eight. Written to grade using simplified language and vocabulary, **science** concepts are more accessible to students and easier for them to understand. Comprised of reading passages, student activities and overhead transparencies, our resource can be used effectively for whole-class, small group and independent work.

How Is Our Resource Organized?

STUDENT HANDOUTS

Reading passages and **activities** (*in the form of reproducible worksheets*) make up the majority of our resource. The reading passages present important grade-appropriate information and concepts related to the topic. Included in each passage are one or more embedded questions that ensure students are actually reading and understanding the content.

For each reading passage there are BEFORE YOU READ activities and AFTER YOU READ activities. As with the reading passages, the related activities are written using a remedial level of language.

- The BEFORE YOU READ activities prepare students for reading by setting a purpose for reading. They stimulate background knowledge and experience, and guide students to make connections between what they know and what they will learn. Important concepts and vocabulary are also presented.
- The AFTER YOU READ activities check students' comprehension of the concepts presented in the reading passage and extend their learning. Students are asked to give thoughtful consideration of the reading passage through creative and evaluative short-answer questions, research, and extension activities.

Hands-on activities are included to further develop students' thinking skills and understanding of the concepts. The **Assessment Rubric** (*page 4*) is a useful tool for evaluating students' responses to many of the activities in our resource. The **Comprehension Quiz** (*page 48*) can be used for either a follow-up review or assessment at the completion of the unit.

PICTURE CUES

Our resource contains three main types of pages, each with a different purpose and use. A **Picture Cue** at the top of each page shows, at a glance, what the page is for.

 Teacher Guide
- Information and tools for the teacher

 Student Handout
- Reproducible worksheets and activities

 Easy Marking™ Answer Key
- Answers for student activities

EASY MARKING™ ANSWER KEY

Marking students' worksheets is fast and easy with this **Answer Key**. Answers are listed in columns – just line up the column with its corresponding worksheet, as shown, and see how every question matches up with its answer!

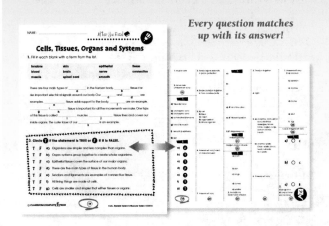

Every question matches up with its answer!

Bloom's Taxonomy

Our resource is an effective tool for any SCIENCE PROGRAM.

Bloom's Taxonomy* for Reading Comprehension

The activities in our resource engage and build the full range of thinking skills that are essential for students' reading comprehension and understanding of important science concepts. Based on the six levels of thinking in Bloom's Taxonomy, and using language at a remedial level, information and questions are given that challenge students to not only recall what they have read, but move beyond this to understand the text and concepts through higher-order thinking. By using higher-order skills of application, analysis, synthesis and evaluation, students become active readers, drawing more meaning from the text, attaining a greater understanding of concepts, and applying and extending their learning in more sophisticated ways.

Our resource, therefore, is an effective tool for any Science program. Whether it is used in whole or in part, or adapted to meet individual student needs, our resource provides teachers with essential information and questions to ask, inspiring students' interest, creativity, and promoting meaningful learning.

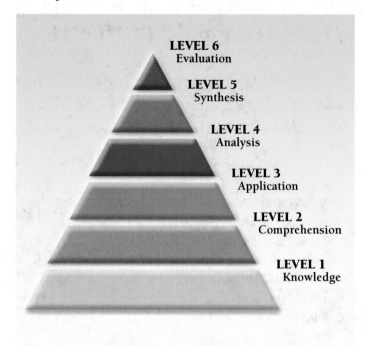

**BLOOM'S TAXONOMY:
6 LEVELS OF THINKING**

Bloom's Taxonomy is a widely used tool by educators for classifying learning objectives, and is based on the work of Benjamin Bloom.

Vocabulary

unicellular	multicellular	specialized cells	nucleus	cytoplasm
mitochondria	lysosomes	cell membrane	epithelial tissue	connective tissue
muscle tissue	nerve tissue	digestive system	circulatory system	reproductive system
muscular system	excretory system	nervous system	oxygen	carbondioxide
electrical signal	spinal cord	blood vessels	nutrients	calcium
marrow	joint rotation	cartilage	cardiac	striated
bundled	muscle fiber	voluntary	involuntary	contracting

Cells – The Building Blocks of Life

1. Complete each sentence with a word from the list. Use a dictionary to help you.

unicellular organisms	multicellular organisms	specialized
bacteria	cells	microscope

a) Every living thing is made up of _____. That is why they are called the building blocks of life.

b) Some living things are very simple. The ones that are only one cell in size are called _____.

c) _____ are an example of unicellular organisms.

d) Humans and frogs are an example of _____.

e) Most cells are very small. We have to use a _____ to be able to see them.

2. Use the cell shapes below to list anything you already know about cells and some questions you have about cells.

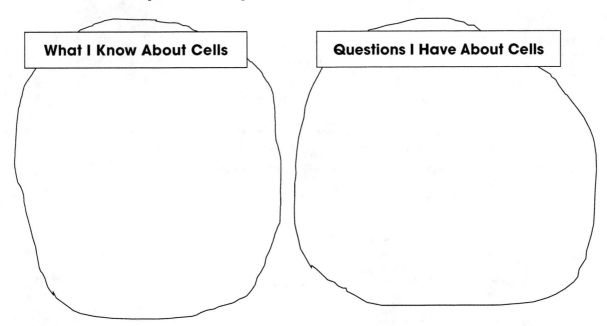

What I Know About Cells

Questions I Have About Cells

Cells – The Building Blocks of Life

Cells are called the building blocks of life because every living thing in the world is made of cells.

Unicellular Organisms

Some living things are very simple and are only one cell in size. These are called **unicellular organisms.** This one cell is able to do all the things needed to keep the organism healthy and alive. The cell can move, eat, breathe, remove waste and reproduce. There are many unicellular organisms in the world but most are far too small to see without a **microscope. Amoeba** and **bacteria** are examples of unicellular organisms. The largest unicellular organism is the ostrich egg!

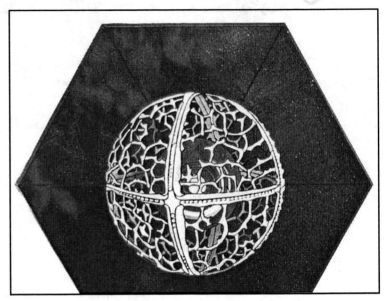

Multicellular Organisms

Almost all of the living things we see around us are **multicellular organisms.** They are made of more than one cell. Every plant and animal, including humans, are multicellular organisms. Some multicellular organisms are only a few cells but most are **billions** of cells. Did you know that a baby is born with 26 billion cells, but by the time it is an adult it will be made of close to 100 trillion cells!

Cells that make up multicellular organisms are **specialized.** They do only certain jobs and need all the other cells to do their own specialized jobs too. Working together, all the cells keep the organism alive and healthy. For example, the cells in our eyes help us see but cannot help us breathe. We need the cells in our lungs for that.

Look around you. List FIVE things you see that are made of cells. Tell whether each thing is UNICELLULAR or MULTICELLULAR.

STOP

_____

_____

_____

NAME: _____

Cells – The Building Blocks of Life

1. Fill in each blank with a term from the list.

alive	amoeba	specialized	multicellular organisms
microscope	billions	unicellular organisms	bacteria
humans	cell	different	

Some living things are very simple and are only one _____ in size. These are
                                                          a

called _____. These are very small and in most cases can only be seen with
         b

a _____. Two examples of unicellular organisms are _____ and
   c   **d**

_____. _____ make up most of the living things that we can see
   e   **f**

around us. Every plant and animal, including _____, are multicellular organisms.
                                              g

They get their name because they are made of more than one cell. This is one way t

hat they are _____ from unicellular organisms. Most multicellular organisms are
             h

made of _____ of cells. These cells are also all very _____. This means
        i   **j**

they have certain jobs to help keep the organism _____.
                                                  k

2. a) <u>Underline</u> the terms and ideas that describe *unicellular* organisms.

simple	human	bacteria	made of billions of cells	ostrich egg
the cells are specialized	tree	made of only one cell	amoeba
so small you need a microscope to see it			

b) Ⓒircle the terms and ideas that describe *multicellular* organisms.

simple	human	bacteria	made of billions of cells	ostrich egg
the cells are specialized	tree	made of only one cell	amoeba
so small you need a microscope to see it			

Cells - The Building Blocks of Life

3. Why are cells considered the building blocks of life?

_____

_____

4. How can a unicellular organism eat, move and breathe when it is only one cell in size?

_____

_____

5. Which statements describe multicellular organisms and which statements describe unicellular organisms? Color the cell that matches the statement.

Feature	Unicellular Organism	Multicellular Organism
a) These living things are very simple	◯	◯◯
b) Every plant and animal is this	◯	◯◯
c) The cells of this organism are specialized	◯	◯◯
d) Most of these organisms are too small to see without a microscope	◯	◯◯
e) Amoeba and bacteria are examples	◯	◯◯
f) You are an example	◯	◯◯

Research

6. Cancer is a disease that affects humans. It is caused by the uncontrolled growth and spread of cells in the body. Your task is to investigate cancer in humans. Collect information about **cancer cells** (What do they look like? How do they grow? How do they harm the human body?). Then, find out some of the most common **treatments.** Write your findings in a one-page report. Include pictures that you find of cancer cells, or illustrate them.

7. Tap water is treated so that humans will be safe from harmful unicellular organisms that may live in it. Find out where the tap water in your home comes from (i.e., a nearby lake? an underground reservoir?). Then find out how the tap water in your area is treated. List some of the main unicellular organisms that this treatment protects you from. You can look for your information on the Internet. Or, you may need to ask your teacher to help you contact someone who works for your town or city in water treatment.

NAME: _____

Cell Structures and Functions

1. Complete each sentence with a word from the list. Use a dictionary to help you.

DNA	nucleus	cytoplasm
cell membrane	lysosomes	mitochondria

a) The liquid inside a cell is called _____.

b) One of the most important parts of a cell is called the _____ because it controls everything the cell does.

c) The nucleus contains special information called _____. This hereditary information helps the cell to reproduce itself.

d) The outside covering of a cell is called the _____.

e) The _____ are the parts of the cell that help break down waste to keep the cell clean and healthy.

f) The _____ helps break down the food we eat so it can be used by the cell.

2. Label the diagram using the terms in the list.

cell	nucleus	cell membrane	cytoplasm

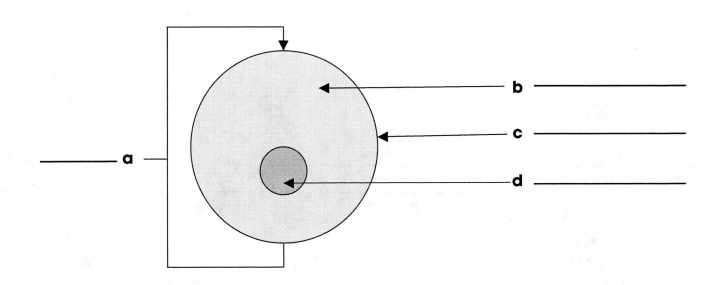

NAME: _____

Cell Structures and Functions

C ells are many different shapes. They can be long like sticks, round like balloons or rectangular like building blocks. Cells are like a factory because they have many parts that work together to get important work done. In the chart below, we use the idea of a factory to help you remember the main parts and what they do.

Cell Part	Where Is It?	What It Does	Job in the Factory
cell membrane	Surrounds the cell	• Separates the inside of the cell from its **environment** • Some elements are let in, some are kept out	• The factory wall or fence
cytoplasm	Inside the cell membrane	• Made of water and **protein**, where most of the cell work takes place	• The busy work space inside the factory
nucleus	Floating in the cytoplasm	• Controls the cell and stores the hereditary information for the cell (**DNA**)	• The factory manager, in charge of all the important activity and information
mitochondria	Floating in the cytoplasm	• Works to turn the food we eat into energy for the cell	• The cooks in the factory cafeteria making lunch for all the other workers
lysosomes	Floating in the cytoplasm	• Break down unneeded parts of the cell	• The factory janitor who keeps things clean

STOP

What is the OUTSIDE part of a cell? Why is it important?

_____

_____

Cell Structures and Functions

1. **Use your knowledge from this reading, as well as the previous reading to complete this activity. <u>Cut out</u> and <u>sort</u> the descriptions at the bottom of the page. Glue them in the correct "cell" that matches each label.**

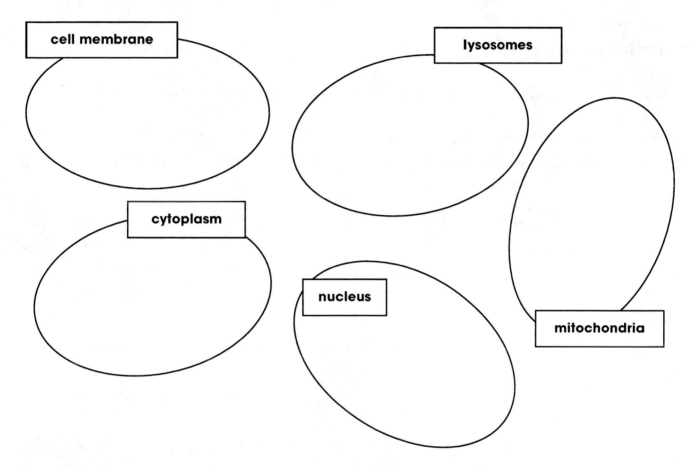

cell membrane

lysosomes

cytoplasm

nucleus

mitochondria

Cell Part Descriptions

A I surround the outside of the cell	**B** This is where all the work takes place – like the inside of a factory	**C** We help keep the cell clean	**D** I float in the cytoplasm
E I float in the cytoplasm, too!	**F** Wow! It's crowded in here! I float in the cytoplasm, too!	**G** I'm like the factory wall – I let things in and keep things out	**H** I help turn the food you eat into what the cell needs to survive
I This is where the DNA is stored	**J** I am made of water and protein	**K** I'm like the manager of the cell – I am in charge of everything!	**L** This is the liquid inside the cell

Cell Structures and Functions

2. What are some of the shapes cells can be?

_____

_____

3. Why is the idea of a factory a good one to understand cell functions?

_____

_____

4. Here are some new words from the reading. Write each word beside its meaning. Use a dictionary to help.

| DNA | environment | protein | hereditary | elements |

_____

a) All of the things and conditions in the surroundings

_____

b) Passing from parents to offspring (children) – eye color is an example of this

_____

c) Similar to "things"; the most basic parts that make up something

_____

d) The material inside the nucleus that stores hereditary information

_____

e) A material we get from food that is necessary for human life to exist

Extension & Application

5. Look at the **cell diagram** on the next page. Use the Internet or books from the library to find a diagram like this one. Use the information you find to **label the parts of the cell** on the diagram.

6. There are more parts in a cell than the ones discussed in the reading. These include: **ribosomes, golgi bodies** and **endoplasmic reticulum**. Do some research to find important facts about **at least one** of these cell structures. Where are they located in the cell? What do they look like? What important job do they do? Include a labeled diagram or illustration with the cell parts in it.

Parts of the Cell

a)_____

b)_____

c)_____

d)_____

e)_____

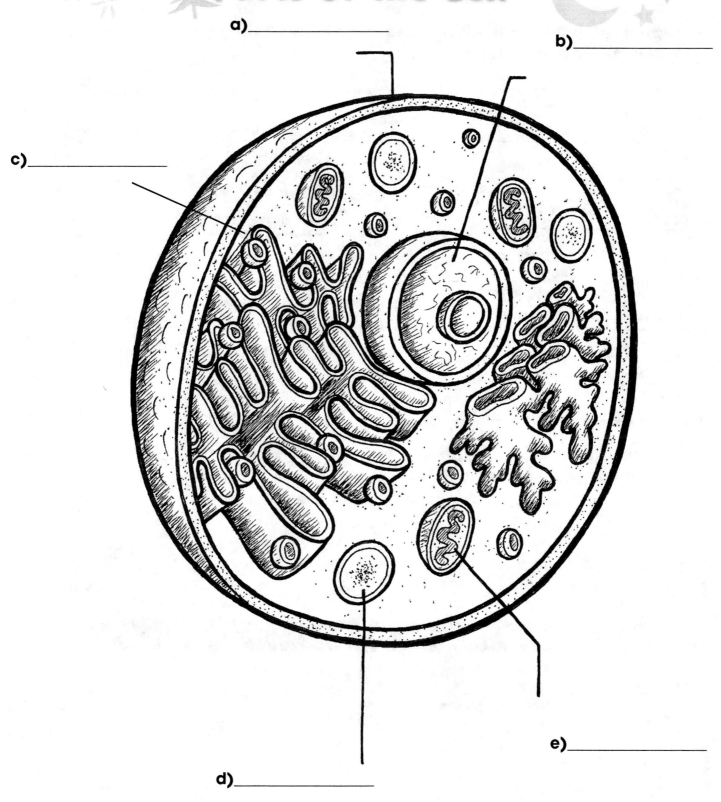

Cells, Skeletal System & Muscular System CC4516

Cells, Tissues, Organs and Systems

1. Match the word on the left to the definition on the right. You may want to use a dictionary to help.

organ	**A** Something that is made of many different parts or units
nerves	**B** A group of cells that have a similar job to do
complex	**C** A group of tissues that have a specialized job (the heart is one of these)
tissue	**D** A single living thing made of many systems (a human being is an example of this)
simple	**E** These carry electrical messages between the brain and other parts of the body
organism	**F** Something that is not complicated or complex

2. The things listed here are ones we have studied so far. Sort them into <u>two</u> groups – those you think are simple and those you think are complex. Write your answers in the chart. Remember, you can use a dictionary to help.

unicellular organism	amoeba	multicellular organism	bacteria
cell	human	system	organ

Simple	Complex

Cells, Tissues, Organs and Systems

How Do Cells Make up an Organism?

How do tiny cells come together to form animals and plants? In most multicellular organisms, whether it is a cat, an elephant or a human, smaller (**simple**) parts join together to create bigger (**complex**) parts.

A way to understand this is to think of the parts of a sandwich – it takes bread, cheese, cold cuts and lettuce to make a ham and Swiss on rye. The simple things (meat and bread) were put together to make the more complex thing (your lunch!). The chart below shows you, step-by-step, how multicellular organisms are organized from simple cells to form complex organisms.

Cellular Level	All living things are made of **cells**.
⬇	
Tissue Level	**Cells** group together to form **tissues**.
⬇	
Organ Level	**Tissues** group together to form **organs**.
⬇	
Organ System Level	**Organs** group together to form **organ systems**.
⬇	
Whole Organism	**Organ systems** group together to form **whole organisms**.

1. Which is SIMPLER? Circle your answers.

   a) organ   organism   **b)** tissue   cell

2. Which is more COMPLEX? Circle your answers.

   a) tissue   organ   **b)** organ system whole organism

Cells, Tissues, Organs and Systems

What Are Tissues?

 T **issue** is a group of cells that work together in the organism to do a specialized job. There are **four main tissue types** in the human body.

The chart below shows what each of these types of tissue do and where they are found.

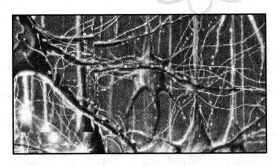

Tissue Type	What It Does	Examples
epithelial tissue	• Covers and lines the surfaces of major organs • Helps keep these organs separate, in place and protected	• Outer layer of skin • Inside lining of the digestive system
connective tissue	• Gives support and structure to the body	• Inner layers of skin, tendons and ligaments • Strange as it may seem, blood is a type of connective tissue, too!
muscle tissue	• Specialized tissue that can change size by **contracting** (shortening) and **flexing** (lengthening). • Allows the body to move	• Smooth muscles (inside lining of organs) • Skeletal muscles (attached to bones) • Cardiac muscles (in the heart)
nerve tissue	• Carries messages, in the form of electrical signals, through the body	• Brain • Spinal cord • Nerves

1. What do you think MUSCLE TISSUE is made of?

_____

2. What do you think NERVE TISSUE is made of?

_____

Cells, Tissues, Organs and Systems

1. Fill in each blank with a term from the list.

tendons	skin	epithelial	tissue
blood	brain	nerve	connective
muscle	spinal cord	smooth	

There are four main types of _____ in the human body. _____ tissue carries
                                        a   **b**

important electrical signals around our body. Our _____ and _____ are
                                                            c   **d**

examples. _____ tissue adds support to the body. _____ are an example.
                    e   **f**

So is _____ ! _____ tissue is important for all the movements we make. One
         g   **h**

type of this tissue is called _____ muscles. _____ tissue lines and covers
                                      i   **j**

our inside organs. The outer layer of our _____ is an example.
                                                    k

2. (Circle) **T** if the statement is TRUE or **F** if it is FALSE.

T   F   **a)**   Organisms are simpler and less complex than organs.

T   F   **b)**   Organ systems group together to create whole organisms.

T   F   **c)**   Epithelial tissue covers the surface of our major organs.

T   F   **d)**   There are five main types of tissue in the human body.

T   F   **e)**   Tendons and ligaments are examples of connective tissue.

T   F   **f)**   All living things are made of cells.

T   F   **g)**   Cells are smaller and simpler than either tissues or organs.

After You Read

Cells, Tissues, Organs and Systems

3. Why is epithelial tissue important to the health of major organs?

_____

_____

4. What is the difference between simple parts and complex parts of an organism?

_____

_____

5. In the flow chart below, list these five levels in order from simplest on the left to most complex on the right: **organism, organ, tissue, cell, organ system**

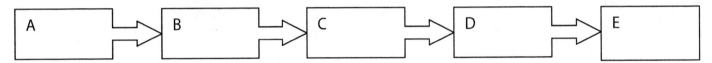

| A | B | C | D | E |

SIMPLEST   **MOST COMPLEX**

Extensions & Applications

6. Human body tissues and plant tissues have **similarities** and **differences**. Investigate both kinds of tissue. Record your findings in a Venn diagram like the one below comparing and contrasting each.

Human Body Tissues   **Plant Tissues**

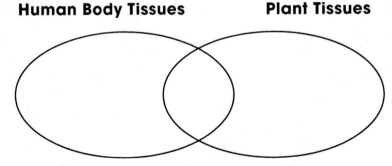

7. We have read about the ideas of "simple" and "complex". These ideas apply to many different things. Make a list of all the food dishes you eat at your favorite holiday meal. What are the **simple ingredients** that make up the **different dishes**? What dishes make up the **meal**? Record your ideas in a chart that shows how simple ingredients are put together to make dishes, and dishes are put together to make a complex meal.

What are Organs and Organ Systems?

1. You be the teacher! Someone has matched the word on the left to the definition on the right. Are they correct? If **yes,** mark it correct with a check mark in the box beside each. If **no,** write an X in the box and correct the work by drawing an arrow to the correct definition. You may use a dictionary to help.

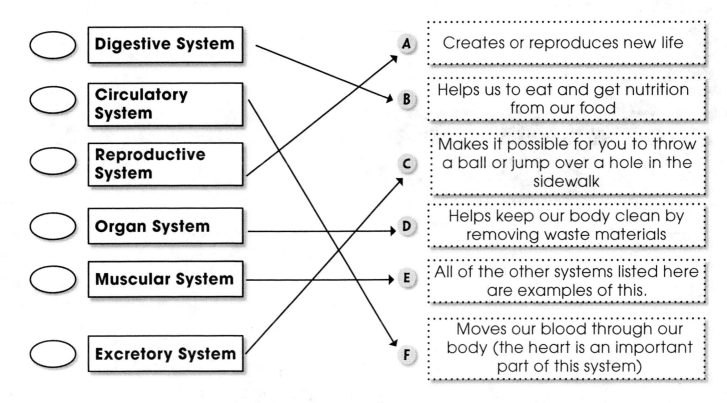

Digestive System	A — Creates or reproduces new life
Circulatory System	B — Helps us to eat and get nutrition from our food
Reproductive System	C — Makes it possible for you to throw a ball or jump over a hole in the sidewalk
Organ System	D — Helps keep our body clean by removing waste materials
Muscular System	E — All of the other systems listed here are examples of this.
Excretory System	F — Moves our blood through our body (the heart is an important part of this system)

2. In the chart below, write **at least one** thing that you know about each of these body systems. You may use a dictionary to help.

Body System	What I Know
Skeletal System	
Nervous System	
Digestive System	
Muscular System	
Respiratory System	

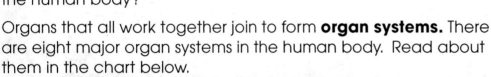

What are Organs and Organ Systems?

Groups of tissue that work together join to form the many different **organs** in the human body. These organs include the liver, kidneys, heart and eyes. Even our skin is an organ. In fact, did you know that the skin is the largest organ in the human body?

Organs that all work together join to form **organ systems.** There are eight major organ systems in the human body. Read about them in the chart below.

Organ System	What It Does
Skeletal	• The **bones** that make up the skeleton support and protect the body
Muscular	• **Muscles** allow the body to move • Muscles also help the materials *inside* the body to move
Circulatory	• **Blood** moves nutrients and wastes around the body • The **heart** pumps which makes the blood move
Nervous	• The **brain** sends electrical messages along the **spinal cord** and **nerves** • These messages tell the body what to do
Respiratory	• Our **lungs** are the main part of the respiratory system • When we **breathe** *in,* a **gas** called **oxygen** goes into our lungs • When we breathe *out,* a waste gas called **carbon dioxide** leaves our body
Digestive	• Breaks down all food taken into the body when we eat • The **nutrients** in food are used to keep us alive and healthy
Excretory	• Removes **waste** materials from the body
Reproductive	• Creates new life through **sexual reproduction**

The job of the respiratory system is to move TWO main gases. What are these two gases?

_____   _____

NAME: _____

What are Organs and Organ Systems?

1. Use the terms in the box to answer each question. Some terms will be left over.

carbon dioxide	skin	bones	lungs	brain
wastes	nutrients	blood	eyes	

_____ **a)** This organ is an important part of the nervous system because it sends messages to all other parts of the body. What is it?

_____ **b)** What is the largest organ in the human body?

_____ **c)** These have the important job of exchanging gases in our body. What are they?

_____ **d)** What is the main part of the skeletal system?

_____ **e)** Our excretory system removes this from our body in order to keep us alive. What is it?

2. In the chart below, list **at least one** way that each body system has helped you today. Once you are done, compare your answers with a classmate.

Organ System	How this System has Helped Me Today
Skeletal	
Muscular	
Circulatory	
Nervous	
Respiratory	
Digestive	
Excretory	

What are Organs and Organ Systems?

3. How do groups of tissues become organs?

_____

_____

4. How many major organ systems are there in the human body?

_____

_____

5. a) Underline the terms that relate to the nervous system. Circle the terms that relate to the respiratory system. Be careful! Not all the terms apply.

muscles	oxygen	sexual reproduction	brain	spinal cord
lungs	bone	electrical messages	carbon dioxide	food
breath	nerves			

b) Underline the terms that relate to the excretory system. Circle the terms that relate to the circulatory system. Be careful! Not all the words apply, and one word applies to *both systems*. **Put a box** around this term.

bones	brain	waste	blood	carbon dioxide	lungs
oxygen	heart	skeleton	nutrients	sexual reproduction	

Extension & Application

6. Using the information from this lesson and your own research, decide which organ should get the **"Most Valuable Organ" Award**. Create a poster celebrating this award and include all the reasons why this organ is the winner. Make sure to include a picture of the winning organ, too!

The Skeletal System – Bones

1. Use your dictionary to look up the meanings of the words below. Write the definition in the space beside each word.

compact	
marrow	
support	
spongy	
protection	
layer	

2. Complete each sentence with a word from the list. Use a dictionary to help you.

bones	skeleton	skull	ribs	marrow	calcium

a) _____ is a mineral in bone that makes it strong.

b) Our system of bones is called our _____.

c) Red blood cells are created deep inside our bones in the
_____.

d) You cannot *see* your _____ because they are under your
skin – but you can *feel* them.

e) Our _____ is the bone that protects our brain.

f) Important organs like our heart and lungs are kept safe behind our
_____

NAME: _____

The Skeletal System – Bones

All of the bones in your body make up your **skeleton**. Your skeleton is also called the **skeletal system**.

STOP

> **1. Write TWO things you know about bones or your skeleton.**
>
> _____
>
> **2. Write a QUESTION that you have about bones or your skeleton.**
>
> _____

You have probably never seen any of your bones, but you can feel their hardness through your skin. It's this hardness that allows bones to do two important jobs: give **support** and give **protection**. The skeleton gives the body structure and support like the veins in an umbrella. Without bones humans would not be able to move, run or even stand. Bones also protect other parts of our body. For example, the brain is protected by the skull; the liver, heart and lungs are covered by the ribs; and the spinal cord is inside the back bones.

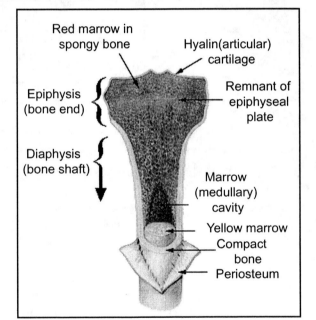

Red marrow in spongy bone
Hyalin (articular) cartilage
Epiphysis (bone end)
Remnant of epiphyseal plate
Diaphysis (bone shaft)
Marrow (medullary) cavity
Yellow marrow
Compact bone
Periosteum

The Parts of a Bone

All bones are made of living cells, blood **vessels** and nerves. They usually have *three layers*:

Compact Bone: The first, outside layer is thin, strong and hard bone. This compact bone contains calcium which makes it tough.

Spongy Bone: The second, middle layer has many tiny holes and looks like "cleaning sponge". The holes allow spongy bone to be strong, but not too heavy.

Bone Marrow: The third, inside layer is made of a soft jelly-like substance called bone marrow. This is where red blood cells are made.

STOP

> **3. In your own words, write ONE thing you have learned about bones or the skeleton. Write your answer in a complete sentence.**
>
> _____

After You Read

The Skeletal System – Bones

1. Put a check mark (✓) next to the answer that is most correct.

a) Why is it important that bones are hard?

- ○ **A** to give our body support
- ○ **B** to keep our muscles strong
- ○ **C** to give us support and protection
- ○ **D** so it is easier to make red blood cells

b) Bone marrow is the third inside layer of bone. What does bone marrow do?

- ○ **A** give our body strength
- ○ **B** protects the rest of the bone
- ○ **C** creates red blood cells
- ○ **D** creates calcium

c) What is the skeletal system made of?

- ○ **A** bones and muscles
- ○ **B** bones
- ○ **C** bones and veins
- ○ **D** bones and the brain

2. Here is a picture of a bone. It shows each of the **three layers** that we have learned about. **Label** each layer with the correct name.

bone marrow   **compact bone**   **spongy bone**

a) _____

b) _____

c) _____

The Skeletal System - Bones

3. What are the three layers of bone?

_____

_____

_____

4. The middle layer of our bones is light. What would happen if it was heavy instead?

_____

_____

5. What are three organs that are protected by the ribs? Can you think of a fourth organ that is also protected by the ribs?

_____

_____

Extension & Application

6. Humans are **protected** by their skeleton. A turtle is protected by a hard shell. In this way, it does the same job as a skeleton. Do some research to learn more about a turtle's shell and the human skeleton. Then, **compare** the skeleton and a turtle's shell. How are they similar and how are they different? Here are some questions for you to consider as you collect your facts:

● **What do they look like?**

● **Where is each located in the body (i.e., on the inside or on the outside?)**

● **What other job or jobs, besides protection, does each do?**

● **How do they grow?**

● **What do they need to stay healthy?**

Present your findings as a one-page report. Add pictures if you like.

7. Do some research to find out **three diseases** that affect the bones in the human body. Also, look for information on ways to keep our bones **healthy**. Copy this T-chart into your notebook. Complete the chart with the information you collect. Share your findings with a classmate.

<u>3 Diseases of the Bones</u> | <u>3 Ways to Keep the Bones Healthy</u>

The Skeletal System – Joints and Cartilage

1. **Circle** the word that completes the sentence. You may use your dictionary to help.

a) The bones of the skeletal system are held together by _____.

joints   **skin**

b) The elbow and knee are examples of _____ joints because they can swing forward and backwards, just like a door.

handle   **hinge**

c) A ball and _____ joint is called this because the ball of one bone fits into the hollow area of the other bone.

soccer   **socket**

d) Our wrists can turn in a complete circle, moving in all directions. This is called _____.

relocation   **rotation**

e) The ends of our bones are protected by a rubbery material called _____.

cytoplasm   **cartilage**

f) The ends of our bones need protection or they wear down from _____ on each other.

banging   **grinding**

2. In the chart below, list what you already know about the skeletal system and some questions you have.

What I Know about the Skeletal System	Questions I Have about the Skeletal System

The Skeletal System – Joints and Cartilage

What Are Joints?

Your skeletal system is made up of an amazing 206 different bones. Bones are connected to each other by **joints.** Without joints, bones would not be able to move because it is at the joint that movement takes place. Three of the most important joints are the ball and socket, hinge and sliding joints.

1. Ball and Socket Joint: This kind of joint allows movement in *almost any direction*, like a computer joystick. Ball and socket joints are found in the shoulder and the hip.

2. Hinge Joint: This type of joint allows for *forward* and *backward* movement, like the hinge of a door. Elbows and knees are hinge joints. A hinge joint does not allow for as much movement as a ball and socket, but it is stronger.

3. Sliding Joint: This type of joint lets bones *slide* easily across each other. This allows both bending and turning (rotation). Ankles and wrists have sliding joints.

Nonaxial
Uniaxial
Biaxial
Multiaxial

ⓕ Ball and socket joint

 **STOP**

Think of all the places in your body where bones join together to form joints. Besides elbows and knees, what is another joint that might be a HINGE JOINT? (Remember how a hinge joint moves...)

_____

_____

What Is Cartilage?

The ends of many bones are covered with a tough rubbery material called **cartilage**. One of the main jobs of cartilage is to protect bones at the joint. Without cartilage, bones would grind against each other when we move them. In time the bones would wear away. Besides our joints, did you know that our ears and the tips of our nose are cartilage, too?

Here is another interesting fact about cartilage: Did you know that most of the twenty-nine bones in your skull (head) are held together by joints made of cartilage? These joints can move a bit in babies, but by the time we are fully grown they do not move at all.

Cells, Skeletal System & Muscular System CC4516

After You Read 📖

The Skeletal System – Joints and Cartilage

1. **Circle** **T** if the statement is **TRUE** or **F** if it is **FALSE.**

T F **a)** The human skeleton is made of 406 bones.

T F **b)** The main job of our joints is to help bones to move.

T F **c)** The hip is an example of a hinge joint.

T F **d)** The wrist is an example of a hinge joint.

T F **e)** Cartilage protects bones from grinding against each other when they move.

T F **f)** The shoulder is an example of a ball and socket joint.

T F **g)** A hinge joint is stronger than a ball and socket joint.

T F **h)** There are 29 bones in our skull all joined by cartilage.

T F **i)** Elbows and knees are both hinge joints.

T F **j)** Sliding joints help wrists and ankles move in all directions.

2. **Here are pictures of each kind of <u>joint</u> that we have learned about. <u>Label</u> each picture with the correct name.**

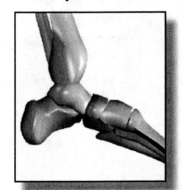 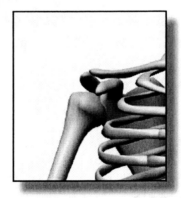 

a) _____

_____

b) _____

c) _____

NAME: _____

The Skeletal System – Joints and Cartilage

3. Why are joints important?

_____

_____

4. What do you think it would be like to walk if we had no cartilage in our leg bones?

_____

_____

5. What joint do you think is the most important and why do you think so?

_____

_____

Research, Extension & Application

6. Humans get slightly **shorter** between adulthood and old age. Do research to find out why this happens.

7. If a hip or knee joint becomes diseased it can be replaced with an **artificial joint**. Do some research to find interesting facts about this surgery. Think about these questions as you collect your facts:
   - **How is a joint replacement done?**
   - **What material is the artificial joint made from? How is it similar to and different from bone?**
   - **What kind of doctor does this surgery?**

8. Every time you take a step your knee joints work. Use a **pedometer** to count the steps you take in a day. Using this number **calculate** how many steps you take in a week (seven days), in a month (30 days) and in a year (365 days).

9. **Calcium** is a mineral important to having strong bones. Research to find **ten foods** high in calcium.

NAME: _____

The Muscular System – Muscles

1. **Match the word on the left to the definition on the right. You may use a dictionary to help.**

bundled	A	This means slender pieces, like threads
cardiac	B	A group of things gathered close together are _____
involuntary	C	This is another word for striped.
striated	D	A word used to describe things related to the heart
fiber	E	Something that happens without thinking about it or choosing it to happen

2. The muscular system has two main jobs. Can you guess what they are? Think about how your body works and what you already know about muscles. Then underline your two guesses from the list below.

muscles help us think faster　　　　　　**muscles help us sleep better**
muscles give our body shape　　　　　　**muscles give us better hearing**
muscles help us move

3. In the chart below list all the things your muscles have helped you to do today. Try to list at least ten different things.

Thanks, muscles! Without you I wouldn't have been able to do any of these things today!
1.
2.
3.
4.
5.
6.
7.
8.
9.
10.

NAME: _____

The Muscular System - Muscles

There are over 600 muscles in the human body. Together they make up the **muscular system.**

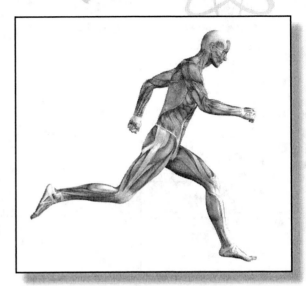

Just like your skeleton, your muscles are below the skin. This means that you can only see the outline of muscles and feel them change shape when they move. Try this – hold your arm up like a weightlifter and tighten your fist. Can you feel the muscles in your upper arm get bigger and harder? Doing this gives you a clue about the two main jobs of muscles:

1. Muscles give our body shape; 2. Muscles help us move. Muscles help us do almost everything – from running on the playground, to pulling the blankets up at night, to breathing in and out.

All muscles in the body are made of cells that are like elastic string. These cells are called **muscle fibers**. Muscle fibers are **bundled** together in groups to form muscles. The number and length of the fibers depend on the size of the muscle.

Three Types of Muscle

There are three types of muscle in the human body. The chart below tells you about them.

Muscle Type	What It Looks Like	How It Moves	What It Does
Skeletal	Striated (striped)	Voluntary (we can control the movement)	Attached to our bones, they allow the bones to move
Smooth	Smooth	Involuntary (we cannot control the movement)	Controls movement inside our body
Cardiac	Striated (striped)	Involuntary (we cannot control the movement)	Allows our heart to pump blood

STOP

What surprising thing have you learned about muscles? Why were you surprised?

_____

_____

NAME: _____

The Muscular System – Muscles

1. (Circle) **T** if the statement is **TRUE** or **F** if it is **FALSE.**

T   F   a)   The human body has over 1000 muscles.

T   F   b)   Muscles help us move.

T   F   c)   Cardiac muscle is voluntary muscle.

T   F   d)   Every human muscle is made of one large muscle fiber.

T   F   e)   If something is "involuntary" it means we cannot control it.

T   F   f)   The human body has three important muscles on top of the skin.

T   F   g)   Muscles give our body shape.

T   F   h)   Striated muscles look like stripes.

T   F   i)   Cardiac muscles are involuntary muscles that help pump our blood.

2. Fill in each blank with a word from the list. There will be two words left over.

bundled	shape	three	cells	run	two	fibers
breathe	move	elastic	muscles			

Muscles have _____ main jobs. They give our body _____ and
                              a   **b**

help us to _____. Without muscles we couldn't _____ or
                        c   **d**

_____. All muscles are made of _____ like _____
              e   **f**   **g**

string. These are called muscle _____. These fibers are _____
                                                          h   **i**

together to create muscles.

The Muscular System – Muscles

3. What are two ways muscles help us?

_____

_____

4. What do skeletal and cardiac muscles look like?

_____

_____

5. What muscle do you think is the most important and why do you think so?

_____

_____

Extension and Application

6. Below is a list of words from the reading. Choose five words that link well together. Then write a **short story** about the day in the life of a muscle. Be imaginative!

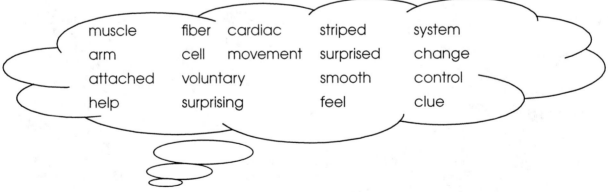

muscle	fiber	cardiac	striped	system
arm	cell	movement	surprised	change
attached	voluntary	smooth	control
help	surprising	feel	clue

7. Using the Internet or books from the library, research **six** different foods that help build healthy muscles. Use these foods to create a **menu** for one day of muscle-healthy eating.

8. **Multiple Sclerosis** is a serious muscle disease. Research important facts about this disease in an encyclopedia or on the Internet. Write a three-paragraph report on the information you find. Try to find out when it was discovered. List its symptoms and treatments.

The Muscular System – Movement

1. Use your dictionary to look up the meaning of the words below. Write the definition in the space beside each word.

voluntary	
tendon	
involuntary	
strain	
esophagus	

2. The body can do each of the things listed below. Decide if each is **voluntary** or **involuntary.** Here's a hint if you get stuck – ask yourself if you can choose to do this thing or if your body does it without you deciding. Write your answers in the chart.

biting an apple	kicking a ball	your heart beating
blood moving in your veins	getting goose bumps at a scary movie	digesting an apple
walking to the bus		

Voluntary	Involuntary

The Muscular System - Movement

We have read that both muscles and bones are both needed for movement. To work together to create movement, muscles and bones have to be connected. Most muscles are attached to bone by strong cords called **tendons**. Tendons look like rubber bands. Besides connecting bone and muscle, one other important job of tendons is to protect muscle from strain during movement.

Can you find any tendons in your body? Try this: Touch the top of your hand as you wiggle your fingers. The hard ridges you feel that run from your fingers to your wrist are tendons.

Upper Arm Muscles

Triceps tendon

Triceps

Biceps tendon

Biceps

Back   Front

Involuntary Muscle Movement

There are two ways that muscles can move. One kind is **involuntary movement**. **Smooth** muscles and **cardiac** muscles both move involuntarily. This means they move on their own; we cannot decide to *make* them move. Our brain sends messages to these muscles "telling" them when they need to move. This happens without us even knowing our muscles are working. An example of involuntary movement is in our digestive system. When we swallow food, the food is pushed down into our stomach by rings of smooth muscles in our **esophagus**. Our stomach is lined with smooth muscle, too. This muscle moves around food we have eaten, breaking it up into small bits so we can get the nutrients from it.

STOP

What are TWO kinds of muscle that move INVOLUNTARILY?

_____

_____

The Muscular System – Movement

One of the most important involuntary muscles is our heart. It is made of cardiac muscle. Cardiac muscle beats, or **contracts,** through our whole life sending blood to every part of our body. On average, the heart beats 70 times a minute. By the time you are 70 years old your heart will have beaten two and a half billion times! Can you imagine if you had to remember to make your heart beat? It would be impossible.

Voluntary Muscle Movement

The second kind of muscle movement is **voluntary.** Voluntary movement happens when we choose to move our muscles; we can control this kind of movement. Three important things come together so we can move. These are our brain, muscles and bones.

Let's look at an example of voluntary muscle movement: It's lunch time and you're hungry. You want to take a big bite of your turkey sandwich. But how does your body get your arm to move to your mouth? The thought, "I'm going to take a bite of my sandwich" causes your brain to send an electrical message through your nerves to two muscles (a pair) your arm. This **muscle pair** works together to move your arm. One muscle in the front of your arm *shortens* (contracts). At the same time the muscle in the back of your arm *lengthens.* This pulls the bone in your lower arm and raises it up towards your mouth. Most skeletal movement happens this way because of the connection of our brain, muscles and bones working together.

Brain, Muscles and Bones Create Voluntary Movement

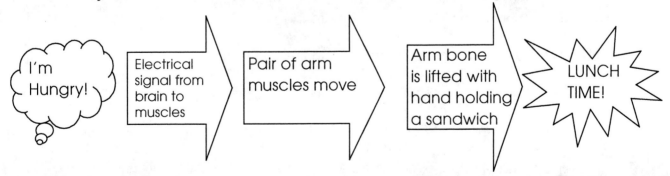

Why is eating a sandwich an example of VOLUNTARY movement?

_____

_____

The Muscular System - Movement

1. Fill in each blank with a word from the list. There will be four words left over.

muscle	arm	voluntary	involuntary	smooth	move
heart	digestive	brain	can	cannot	

Cardiac and _____ muscles are both types of _____
                              a   b
muscles. We_____ control their movement. Our _____ sends
                          c   d
signals to these muscles to make them _____, and we don't even know
                                              e
it is happening. The muscles of our _____ system are involuntary muscles.
                                            f
To make _____ muscles move we have to decide to move them, this is
               g
an example of voluntary muscles.

2. ⬭ Circle **T** if the statement is **TRUE** or **F** if it is **FALSE**.

T   F   a)   Most muscles are attached to bone by a strong cord called ligament.

T   F   b)   Three important things come together in voluntary movement.

T   F   c)   These three important things are the brain, muscles and internal organs.

T   F   d)   When a muscle shortens we call this contracting.

T   F   e)   Involuntary muscles work in pairs to move.

T   F   f)   An example of tendons are the hard ridges that run from our fingers to wrist.

T   F   g)   Smooth muscles and cardiac muscles are both involuntary.

T   F   h)   Tendons help protect muscles from strain.

After You Read 📖

The Muscular System – Movement

3. Why do you think it is important that the heart is an involuntary muscle?

_____

_____

4. Why do you think it is important that the muscles in our legs are voluntary muscles?

_____

_____

5. How do the muscles in your arm work together to create movement?

_____

_____

Extension & Application

6. Using the Internet, research **ten** different **world records** of human movement. Some examples include:

fastest 100 meters   fastest marathon   highest pole vault
highest high jump   fastest 100 meter speed skate
fastest 500 meter breast stroke (swimming)

For each world record, write down whether it is a record for men or women, and list the country that the winner is from.

Record your findings in a chart like the one below.

World Record	Name of Winner	Male or Female?	Country

Most of these world records will be for voluntary muscle movement. Can you find any that are for **involuntary movement?**

Build Your Own Cell

We have learned that human body cells can be different shapes and sizes, but they all have some parts in common.

Do you remember what they are?

1. The **cell membrane** is the outside covering that separates the cell from its environment.

2. The **cytoplasm** is the jelly-like substance inside the cell where all the work takes place.

3. The **nucleus** floats in the cytoplasm and contains DNA.

4. The **mitochondria** float in the cytoplasm too, and turn food into energy.

5. The **lysosomes** also float in the cytoplasm and keep the cell clean.

FOR THIS ACTIVITY, you will need:

- 5 different colors of plasticine
- 5 toothpicks
- small pieces of paper
- tape

STEPS:

1. Use plasticine to **sculpt** your cell. First, decide what shape it will be. Remember that human body cells can be long and thin, round, or rectangular in shape. Use a different **color** for each cell part. The cell should be **at least** the size of your hand.

2. Once you have finished sculpting your cell, place the toothpicks in the plasticine. You will use them as markers for the different cell parts.

3. On a small piece of paper, write down the cell part. "Flag" it by sticking the toothpick in the plasticine.

4. Tape the label (small piece of paper) to the toothpick.

When you are finished, someone should be able to look at your plasticine cell and see the five different parts labeled. Have fun sculpting!

Create a Human Body Organ System Booklet

We have learned that the human body has EIGHT major organ systems. Each system is made up of important ORGANS, and these organs work together as a SYSTEM. All of these organ systems have important jobs to do to keep our body healthy and alive.

Your task is to create a booklet with important facts about each of the organ systems:

skeletal system	muscular system
circulatory system	nervous system
respiratory system	digestive system
excretory system	reproductive system

YOUR BOOKLET SHOULD INCLUDE:

- a cover page with the title of your book
- a Table of Contents page
- at least one page for each organ system

COLLECTING YOUR INFORMATION:

Begin by collecting important **facts** about each system. You may use the reading passages, the Internet, or other resource materials to find your information. For each organ system, try to include the following:

1. **Major organs** that make up the system

2. The **main jobs** of the organ system (what it does)

3. A **picture** that shows what the system looks like (be sure to label all the parts!)

4. Other interesting facts that you find

Invent an Alien Skeleton!

This activity has two parts. For the first part, you will label the bones in the human skeleton. For the second part, you will use what you have learned to invent your own extra-terrestrial skeleton.

Part 1

Use the words in the list to **label** the bones on the skeleton. You may need to do some research to complete this part.

ribs
patella
backbone
pelvis
femur
tibia
scapula
sternum
humerus
fibula
clavicle
radius
phalanges
ulna
mandible

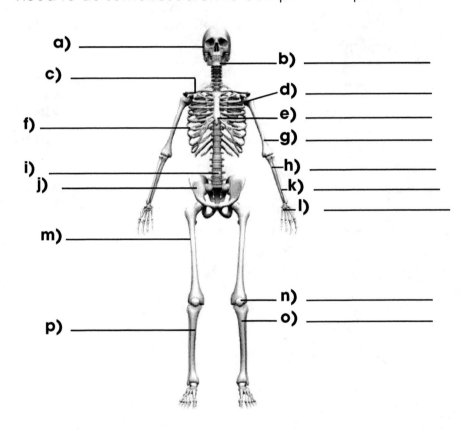

a) _____
b) _____
c) _____
d) _____
e) _____
f) _____
g) _____
h) _____
i)
j) _____
k) _____
l) _____
m) _____
n) _____
o) _____
p) _____

Part 2

Now, it is time to **draw** your own **alien skeleton!** You must use **at least ten** different skeleton parts from the diagram above. You may use the parts more than once if you like. Be as imaginative as you can! Draw your skeleton on a separate sheet of paper. Above your drawing, copy and complete the following:

Hello! I am an extra-terrestrial from the planet _____.

My name is _____ and my favorite food is _____.

I have _____ skulls, _____ femurs, _____ tibias, and _____ ribs.

Pin the Organ on the Body

Below is an outline of the human body. At the left side of the page are pictures of important **ORGANS** in the body. Your task is to **CUT OUT** each organ and **PASTE** it on the body where it belongs. You may use information from the reading passages, the Internet, or other resource materials to find the answers.

a) liver

b) intestines

c) brain

d) bladder

e) heart

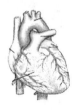

f) lungs

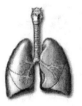

g) stomach

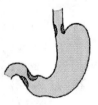

h) kidneys

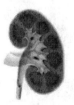

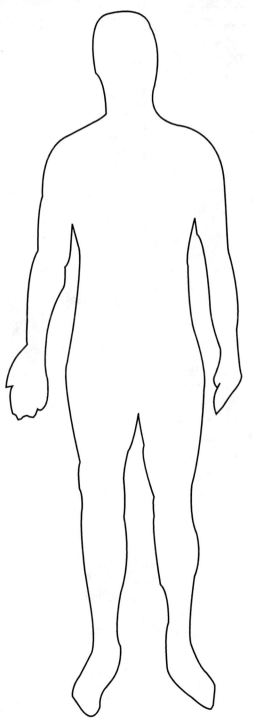

NAME: _____

Crossword Puzzle!

Across

1. Muscle tissue changes size by _____ and lengthening
3. The human body is made of _____ cells
4. Muscle_____ are like elastic string
6. Humans are_____ organisms
8. The knee is an example of a _____ joint
10. _____ muscles allow our bones to move
11. Cells group together to form _____
13. The cell contains special information called _____
14. There are _____ major organ systems in the human body

Down

1. The liquid inside a cell is called _____
2. The skeletal system is made of bones, joints and _____
4. The heart is made of _____ muscle
5. Nerve tissue carries messages from the brain in the form of electrical _____
7. The digestive system is made of mostly _____ muscles
9. Muscles work in _____; one shortens and the other lengthens
12. Mitochondria turn food into _____

Word List

specialized	cytoplasm
contracting	energy
DNA	cardiac
cells	involuntary
tissues	pairs
hinge	cartilage
multicellular	signals
eight	skeletal

NAME: _____

Word Search

Find all of the words in the Word Search. Words are written horizontally, vertically, diagonally, and some are even written backwards.

multicellular
tissue
calcium
specialized
unicellular
marrow
nucleus
organ
compact
cytoplasm
muscle
cartilage
mitochondria
nerve
tendon
lysosomes
skeletal
contract
complex
cardiac
socket
joint
involuntary
hinge
fiber
striated
bundled
rotation

Q	A	Z	X	S	M	C	T	C	A	P	M	O	C	S	W	E	U
P	L	K	S	A	A	D	K	G	O	P	L	M	K	P	S	N	E
W	S	D	R	I	E	D	S	U	E	L	C	U	N	E	I	J	B
S	Y	R	D	H	N	M	J	C	O	N	T	R	A	C	T	K	U
C	O	R	T	G	B	Y	H	N	M	J	U	K	E	I	P	L	M
W	A	C	X	D	S	K	E	L	E	T	A	L	D	A	R	F	X
C	T	L	K	Y	H	N	U	J	M	K	L	E	D	L	T	J	K
B	G	T	C	E	Y	H	N	U	K	U	O	P	H	I	N	G	E
E	D	T	A	I	T	Y	H	N	L	I	U	J	M	Z	I	K	P
W	S	T	R	Y	U	H	N	A	M	N	E	R	V	E	K	G	B
A	Z	D	T	F	G	M	R	H	J	V	T	H	U	D	Y	H	A
U	J	O	I	N	T	Y	L	Y	S	O	S	O	M	E	S	G	I
V	F	R	L	A	G	B	N	M	J	L	K	H	F	I	B	E	R
C	U	J	A	G	J	K	L	M	B	U	N	D	L	E	D	C	D
Y	O	H	G	R	S	T	R	I	A	T	E	D	M	J	K	U	N
T	Q	M	E	O	S	T	R	I	A	T	E	D	U	C	V	B	O
O	T	B	P	Y	E	S	R	O	T	A	T	I	O	N	M	D	H
P	D	C	T	L	T	Y	J	U	K	R	N	K	U	T	G	H	C
L	T	D	C	H	E	I	R	O	T	Y	T	I	O	N	Y	F	O
A	D	S	Z	X	C	X	S	T	G	B	N	N	O	D	N	E	T
S	U	S	D	F	T	H	U	S	D	Y	A	W	E	R	Q	F	I
M	U	L	T	I	C	E	L	L	U	L	A	R	A	Y	G	C	M
D	E	L	D	N	U	B	D	S	X	E	Y	H	N	M	K	U	P

NAME: _____

Comprehension Quiz

 32

Part A

Circle **T** if the statement is TRUE or **F** if it is FALSE.

8

T   F   **1)**   The cell nucleus contains hereditary information called DNA.

T   F   **2)**   In the human body, organs are made of groups of tissue that have a specific job.

T   F   **3)**   Organ systems are simpler than organs.

T   F   **4)**   Three of the major organ systems in the human body are the respiratory system, skeletal system and brain system.

T   F   **5)**   In the circulatory system, the heart pumps blood through our nerves.

T   F   **6)**   The main jobs of the skeletal system is to give protection and support.

T   F   **7)**   The ends of our bones are covered by a rubbery material called cytoplasm.

T   F   **8)**   Skeletal muscles control the digestion of food in our stomach.

Part B

On the diagram below, label the three layers of bone.
Use the words in the list.

 6

bone marrow   **spongy bone**   **compact bone**

1. _____

2. _____

3. _____

SUBTOTAL: **/14**

After You Read

Comprehension Quiz

Part C

Answer each question in complete sentences.

1. What are **specialized cells?** Are they found in unicellular or multicellular organisms? Give an example of an organism that is made of specialized cells.

   3

   _____

   _____

   _____

2. Name **two parts of a cell.** Describe the **function** of each part in the cell.

   4

   _____

   _____

   _____

3. Name **one kind of tissue** in the human body. Describe **what it does** in the body. Give an example of this type of tissue.

   3

   _____

   _____

   _____

4. What is the difference between **voluntary** and **involuntary** movement? Name **one** kind of muscle that moves voluntarily. Name **one** kind of muscle that moves involuntarily.

   4

   _____

   _____

   _____

5. Describe how **voluntary movement** happens. Use the words **brain, muscle pair** and **bone** in your answer.

   4

   _____

   _____

   _____

SUBTOTAL: **/18**

2.
Thin and long, round, rectangular

3.
Like a factory, cells have many parts that work together to get important work done

4.
a) environment
b) hereditary
c) elements
d) DNA
e) protein

5.
a) Cell membrane b) Nucleus
c) Ribosome d) Lysosome
e) Mitochondria

6.
Answers will vary

(14)

1.
cell membrane – **A, G**
lysosomes – **C, D/E/F**
cytoplasm – **B, J, L**
nucleus – **D/E/F, I, K**
mitochondria – **D/E/F, H**

(13)

1.
a) cytoplasm
b) nucleus
c) DNA
d) cell membrane
e) lysosomes
f) mitochondria

2.
a) cell
b) cytoplasm
c) cell membrane
d) nucleus

(11)

Cell membrane – lets some things in, keeps other things out

(12)

3.
All living things are made of cells

4.
It can do everything an organism needs to do to stay alive and healthy

5.

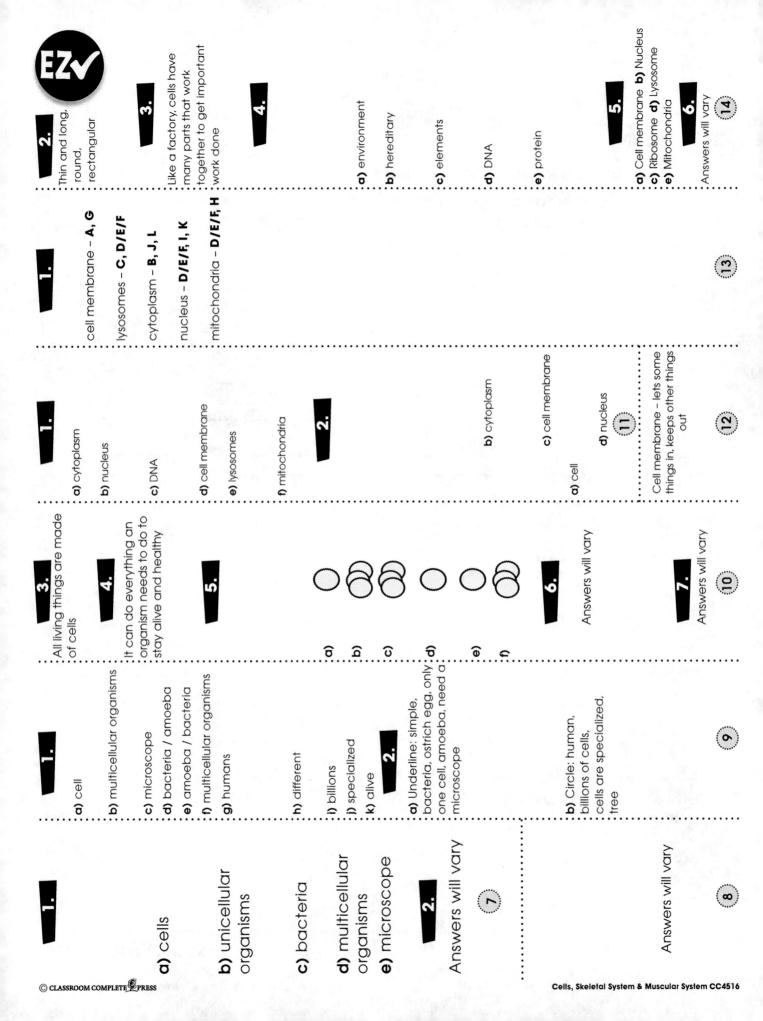

a)
b)
c)
d)
e)
f)

6.
Answers will vary

7.
Answers will vary

(10)

1.
a) cell
b) multicellular organisms
c) microscope
d) bacteria / amoeba
e) amoeba / bacteria
f) multicellular organisms
g) humans
h) different
i) billions
j) specialized
k) alive

2.
a) Underline: simple, bacteria, ostrich egg, only one cell, amoeba, need a microscope

b) Circle: human, billions of cells, cells are specialized, tree

(9)

1.
a) cells
b) unicellular organisms
c) bacteria
d) multicellular organisms
e) microscope

2.
Answers will vary

(7)

Answers will vary

(8)

1. Answers will vary
2. a) calcium
   b) skeleton
   c) marrow
   d) bones
   e) skull
   f) ribs (25)

1, 2, 3. Answers will vary (26)

1.
a) C
b) C
c) B
2.
a) spongy bone
b) compact bone
c) bone marrow (27)

3. They join together

4. Eight

5. a) Underline: brain, spinal cord, electrical messages, nerves
   Circle: oxygen, lungs, carbon dioxide, breath
   b) Underline: waste
   Circle: waste, blood, heart, nutrients
   Box: waste

6. Answers will vary (24)

1.
a) ✓
b) ✓
c) ✓
d) ✗ –All of the other...
e) ✗ –Makes it possible...
f) ✗ –Helps keep our...
2. Answers will vary (21)

Oxygen, carbon dioxide (22)

1.
a) brain
b) skin
c) lungs
d) bones
e) wastes
2. Accept any reasonable answers (23)

3. Keeps organs separate, in place, protected

4. Simple parts join together to form complex parts

5. A) cell
   B) tissue
   C) organ
   D) organ system
   E) Whole organism

6. Answers will vary based on resources used

7. Answers will vary (20)

1. muscle cells

2. nerve cells (Answers will vary) (18)

1.
a) tissue b) nerve
c) brain/spinal cord
d) brain/spinal cord
e) connective f) tendons
g) blood h) muscle
i) smooth j) epithelial
k) skin
2.
a) F
b) T
c) T
d) F
e) T
f) T
g) T
(19)

1.
A) complex
B) tissue
C) organ
D) organism
E) nerves
F) simple
2.
Simple: unicellular organism, amoeba, bacteria, cell
Complex: multicellular organism, human, system, organ
(Answers will vary) (16)

1. a) organ b) cell
2. a) organ b) whole organism (17)

Answers will vary (34)

1.
a) F
b) T
c) F
d) F
e) T
f) F
g) T
h) F
i) T

2.
a) two
b) shape
c) move
d) run/breathe
e) run/breathe
f) cells
g) elastic
h) fibers
i) bundled
(35)

3. Possible answers: Give our body shape, help us move
4. Stripes
5. Answers will vary
6. Answers will vary
7. Answers will vary
8. Answers will vary
(36)

1. Answers will vary

2. Voluntary: biting an apple, kicking a ball, walking to the bus

Involuntary: your heart beating, blood moving in your veins, getting goose bumps at a scary movie, digesting an apple
(37)

3. Allow bones to move
4. Possible answer: difficult, painful
5. Answers will vary
6. Answers will vary
7. Answers will vary
8. Answers will vary
9. Answers will vary
(32)

1.
A) fiber
B) bundled
C) striated
D) cardiac
E) involuntary

2. Give our body shape, Help us move

3. Answers will vary
(33)

1.
a) F
b) T
c) F
d) F
e) T
f) T
g) T
h) F
i) T
j) T

2.
a) sliding joint
b) ball and socket joint
c) hinge joint
(31)

1.
a) joints
b) hinge
c) socket
d) rotation
e) cartilage
f) grinding

2. Answers will vary
(29)

Answers will vary
(30)

3. Outside: compact bone
Middle: spongy bone
Inside: bone marrow

4. Accept any reasonable answer

5. Heart, lungs, liver; Possible fourth organ-stomach (Answers will vary)

6. Answers will vary
(28)

7. Answers will vary

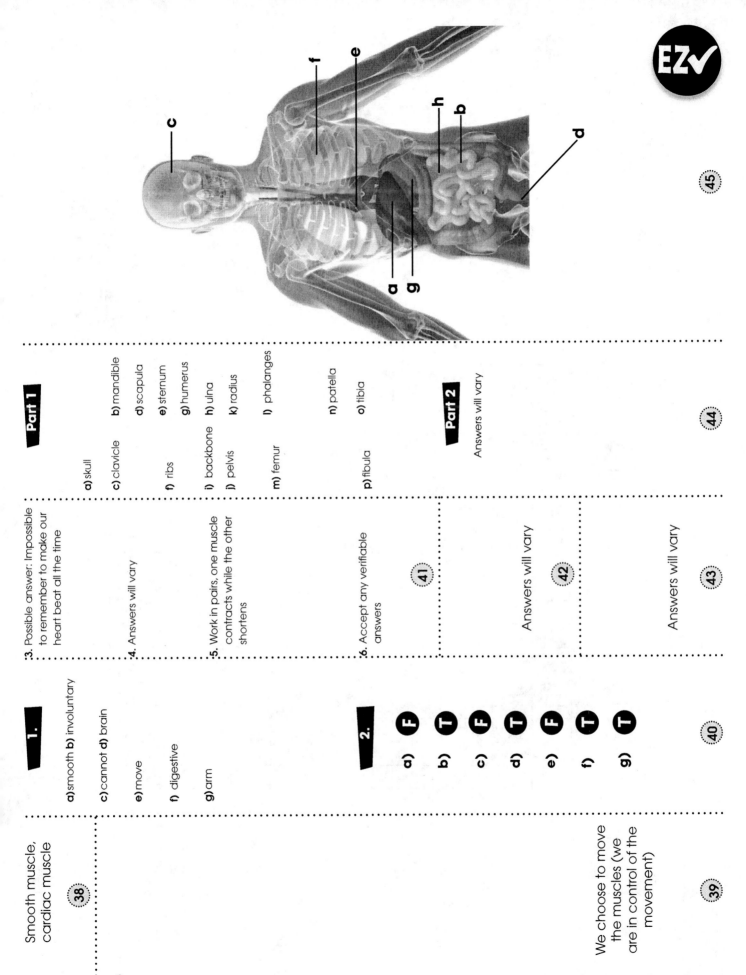

Part 1

a) skull
b) mandible
c) clavicle
d) scapula
e) sternum
f) ribs
g) humerus
h) ulna
i) backbone
j) pelvis
k) radius
l) phalanges
m) femur
n) patella
o) tibia
p) fibula

Part 2

Answers will vary

(44)

(45)

---

3. Possible answer: Impossible to remember to make our heart beat all the time

4. Answers will vary

5. Work in pairs, one muscle contracts while the other shortens

6. Accept any verifiable answers

(41)

Answers will vary

(42)

Answers will vary

(43)

1.

a) smooth b) involuntary
c) cannot d) brain
e) move
f) digestive
g) arm

2.

a) F
b) T
c) F
d) T
e) F
f) T
g) T

(40)

Smooth muscle, cardiac muscle

(38)

We choose to move the muscles (we are in control of the movement)

(39)

Word Search Answers

Across:

1. contracting
3. specialized
4. cells
6. multicellular
8. hinge
10. skeletal
11. tissues
13. DNA
14. eight

Down:

1. cytoplasm
2. cartilage
4. cardiac
5. signals
7. involuntary
9. pairs
12. energy

Part A

1) **T**
2) **T**
3) **F**
4) **F**
5) **F**
6) **T**
7) **F**
8) **F**

Part B

1. spongy bone
2. compact bone
3. bone marrow

Part C

1. Cells that do specific jobs and not other jobs; multicellular; possible example: human

2. Answers will vary

3. Answers will vary

4. **Voluntary –** we can control it, **Involuntary –** we cannot control it. Examples will vary

5. **Possible answer:** We decide to move. The brain sends electrical signal to muscles. Muscle pair moves (one contracts (shortens) and the other lengthens). Bone moves because muscles are working.